The Secret Life of Railroaders

Jim McLean

Coteau Books

For Myrna, a railroader's wife

Table of Contents

3. Wrecking

4. I Don't Write Poems for Railroaders

Canadian Pacific

strange
how in this cold rational country
it seems   reasonable
to love or hate
a railway

1. To Run the Trains

some things you probably didn't know about railroads

The Apache Railway Company
is headquartered in Snowflake, Arizona.

A reefer
is not
what you think it is.

Neither is dope.

A kicker
is either a malfunctioning air brake
an integral part of a freight car coupler
or a trainman who's been held-away more than 12 hours.

There are 84 different reasons
for changing out a pair of freight car wheels.

Black collar is neither
a contagious disease
nor a laundry problem.

There are more than 1,300 railway companies
in North America.

Woodpeckers weigh 300 pounds.

Frogs are twenty feet long.

The Crab Orchard & Egyptian R.R. of Marion, Illinois
owns two locomotives
both coal-burning.

A depressed flat
is not
a late-blooming teenage girl.

"The placing of advertisements or banners of any kind
upon any freight or passenger car or locomotive
is prohibited."

Whoever painted "Keep the Crow"
on one of our boxcars
is in big trouble!

4

A hump yard
is no place to be making love.

A yard of rail weighs 100 pounds.
A pair of wheels about a ton.
A locomotive 200 tons.

The Head-On Collision Line
runs 80 tank cars
out of Chicago.

It is forbidden
to stick railway spikes up your nose.

The Norfolk and Western
owns 96,485 freight cars.

Insecure coupling
occurs more often at drive-in theatres
than on the railway.

The Bangor and Aroostook
is one of my favourite railway names.

A hot box
is exactly
what you think it is.

to run the trains
(read in the style of a steam locomotive)

from a standing start	dead man
	tender man
drivers spinning	pig&goat
	pool
	hogger
	boomer
	blue-flag-rule
steadier, gaining purchase	draw bar
	angle bar
	piggy-back hitch
momentary wheel slippage	ree fer
	ditch lights
	dw-arf switch
pause here to pick up	
a little bit of steam	
a little bit of speed	
	car knocker
faster, increasing in	track walker
speed and regularity	bad order load
	dinger
	first man
	foreign road
	master mechanic
	rush waybill
	Wabco brakes
	& a fish-belly sill
break for crossing whistle	
2 long, 1 short, 1 long	
tempo much faster and	bi-level
	tri-level
	bathtub dump
	underslung pinlift
	"do not hump"
rolling free	time table
	turntable
	A.C.I.
	RR & R
	west leg of the wye

pure speed and power

capacity
light weight
finger gauge
roller bearing
squirrel cage
call
& cancel
book-off sick
mileage 80
cinder dick

distorted ringing of bell
at wig-wag as poem thunders
over level crossing

with speed and confidence

gardens
sump track
symbol train
cross-over pipe
auxiliary crane
high flange
thin flange
scooped in the yard
combo spider
red time card

clickety-clack
clickety-clack
clickety-clack
clickety-clack

quickly, aggressively

now don't give me
no funny looks
if you can't find
these words in books
and all your learning
can't explain
the terms it takes

a sudden pause
before the grinding of brakes
and a great whoosh of steam

to run the trains

so the day begins

the day begins
under the sun's light
or with the rain forming oily serpentines
of metallic green and purple
or with another snowfall to clear

this day is hot
already heat waves
shimmer above the rails
men move to their tools
as they did 6
or 600 or 6,000 days before

the day begins
like a column in a great newspaper
that has never missed a deadline
the words as linear
and never-ending as boxcars
strung out along a prairie horizon
the words
laid end to end
like rails
like long trains of freight cars
that pass through cities
through divisions
through provinces stacked
side by side
like generations
who labour/retire/die
minutes/months/years

the sky
depending on the season

klik

the apprentice from Winnipeg
couldn't stand klik

whenever he found
the marbled pink meat sandwiches
in his lunch kit
he would throw them in the garbage
work the rest of the day
on fruit
tormented by the memory
of lunches mother used to make
peanut butter   bacon & tomato
egg salad

the apprentice from Winnipeg
hated klik

too shy to tell the woman
who packed his lunch each day
he made the mistake
of telling us
and every evening after work
carried home in his lunch pail
a note to his landlady
in bold enthusiastic letters

more klik!
love that klik!

Susan: A True Story

he had to be a bit of an actor
in the first place
hiring on at fifteen
lying about his age

it was getting even
for what he had endured
about his pimples and how he got them
the fool's errands
for pails of blue steam and board-stretchers
the red-faced memory
of that first winter
going into the office
to ask for his Christmas turkey
the humiliation
of their laughter

so he invented the sister
older than he
adding just the right amount of brotherly disdain
for the heady perfume
that followed in her wake
the endlessly washed and hanging nylons
the unjust tolerance
of his father

invented boy friends, too
in suits and sports coats
with clean-cut purring Fords or Oldsmobiles
and college degrees
gave them names like George or Kent
laughed at the way he could sucker them
out of their shining cars
laying rubber and stripping gears
while Kent or Old George sat correctly
in the living room
calling his father sir

hell! a girl like that
deserves a real man
they started wearing
their best ball-jackets to work
fought among themselves
to be his protector
took him everywhere
on their motorcycles

he turned aside
their clumsy requests for introductions
by intense questioning
about throw-out bearings
and 4-speed transmissions
with adolescent cold indifference
refused to discuss her anymore
so that each one invented her again
for himself

it was a game
that had to end
the ending the objective
and when at last they knew
they'd been exposed
it came to pass
that   lifted on their admiration
the boy took his place
among men

Twenty years ago, freight car axles were lubricated by packing them with a combination of fabric waste and thread mixed with oil. This waste or "dope" was reclaimed and cleaned by running it through an extractor. Cleaning dope was a noisy, dirty, boring job, but the gloomy dope room made a great testing ground for a would-be teenage idol.

dope room blues

he shakes out the dope
long stringy oil-soaked handfuls
feeds it into the extractor
as *Little Darlin'* rises above the roar
boop-boop-boop   boop-de-doop
the falsetto coming in with split-second timing
lah-lah-lah-lah   lah-lah
pencil across the teeth
for the starlight strings finale
three quick stomps
and it's over

he looks around   making certain
no one has come in
still half a load left in the wheelbarrow
could do *Don't Be Cruel*
or maybe a Johnny Mathis
decides instead on the harmony for
Ah Wonder If Ah Care As Much
by the Everlys

secure beside the hammering machine
he belts out entire scores
doing all the parts himself
instrumental sections too
uses whatever's handy
tongue   teeth   fingers
even eyelids
remembers a loose pulley belt
keeping perfect time
to *Peggy Sue*

he shuts off the extractor
wipes the oil from his wheelbarrow

took him four full loads
to get *My Prayer* down right

his dream
is to do *Heartbreak Hotel*
inside an empty tank car

Freight cars are switched in blocks or "cuts." A switchman will "pull the pin," uncoupling the cars, and walk up the cut bleeding the air from the brakes. When he reaches the engine, the cut is pulled out and switched to other tracks.

Steam line connectors, or barcos, had to be disconnected between the railway passenger cars before the cars could be uncoupled. Sometimes, switch crews would uncouple the cars and pull them apart before the carman had disconnected the steam line. Needless to say, the barcos would be torn off the cars, and carmen, not switchmen, had to repair them.

advice from an old rail

the next time that sonofabitch
pulls a barco on you
wait until you see him
bleeding a cut in F Yard
then you slip over and pull the pin
two or three cars ahead of his cut

he'll switch the whole damn cut
off his sheet
won't realize what's happened
until he gets down to the last few cars
by then it'll be too late
and he'll have to go back
into every track

don't let him see you, though
he'd break his goddamn neck
gettin' upstairs
to squeal on you

14

the well-equipped carman

steel-toed boots & hard hats
sparkers & goggles & mitts
overalls parkas & flashlights
gaskets & heavy tool kits

pulling hooks & oil cans
tacks & bad-order cards
little black two-way radios
so you won't get lost in the yards

blue flags & steel wheel gauges
3-buckle felt overshoes
itchy woolen underwear
an increase in union dues

temp sticks & ball-peen hammers
it's enough to drive you berserk
& under all of these burdens
you're expected to do some work!

so just hand me that big old shovel
stick a switch broom straight up my ass
I'll plow my way to quittin' time
& pray for the winter to pass

before radio

you listened

       two whistles
       go ahead
       three for back up
       four to get the gate

or looked

       bad order
       blind joint
       set brakes
       two thumbs up   for lunch

could almost
get through a shift
on sign language alone

       three   cars
       two   cars
       one car
       stop (or wipe-out)
       cut off

without a word
a man could make
a perfect join

and
most graphic
of all

       hands coupled
       to make
       a big-belly arc

the signal for
an approaching official

Remembrance Day

BULLETIN NO. 039

SUBJECT:
RE: REMEMBRANCE DAY STATUTORY HOLIDAY
NOV. 11, 1975

Employees will be permitted to observe the two minute silence at eleven o'clock, provided it does not interfere with the normal operation of the trains.

To paraphrase the old saying: you can take the boy out of the
railroad but you can't take the railroad out of the boy.

summer vacation

from Los Angeles International Airport
to Anaheim
takes 55 minutes by bus

he saw some buildings
and the rail yards (Southern Pacific)

pointed out to his wife
freight cars
stencilled with the yellow dot
explained
they had been examined
for 70-ton Southern wheels
8.14 per
Rule 80
job code 4628

saw Disneyland

flew home
L.A. to Calgary
in 2½ hours

the night watch

after doing a graveyard shift
in the rail yards at 40 below
with the steam frozen around my parka
like a second skin
the cold settles in my bones
and chaps my wrists raw
so when the day boys finally start to roll in
I'm grateful almost to the point of weary tears
and I remember from high school how well
Shakespeare made the guard in *Hamlet* say

For this relief much thanks   'tis bitter cold
and I am sick at heart

I'm sure the C.P.R. invented Spring

I'm sure the C.P.R. invented Spring
it's just like them to do that sort of thing
when you think that you will crack
swear you're never coming back
to lie down on the ground
in the snow to curse and pound
at those frozen Wabco brakes
till your whole damn body aches
and you start to shout and yell
that you'd rather live in hell—
someone wires Montreal

then the flowers start to bud
the snow melts into mud
and the sun fills up the sky
so dazzling blue you want to cry
and you pity those poor jerks
stuck inside as office clerks
and you tip your hat and sing
to old Van Horne who dreamed up Spring

oh, I'm sure the C.P.R. invented Spring
it's the way they have to keep you on the string
with the robins and the crows
you forget your frozen toes
when the sun begins to shine
why, the trains get back on time
and you settle right back in
forget your oath to pull the pin
decide to have another go
ah, when those summer breezes blow
who minds a little snow?

but pretty soon the leaves begin to fall
and you realize you haven't tried at all
to get a job where you won't freeze
(with a receptionist to squeeze)
teaching English   selling cars
waiting tables in the bars
cooking french fries   anything!
when you feel old winter's sting
you *know* the C.P.R. invented Spring

each year I tell myself that it's the last
when I'm shaking in a January blast
and I can almost see the day
when I'll just quit and walk away
to start my new career
down at Molson's   testing beer
but then I turn and hunch my back
tramp another mile of track
tell myself I'll never leave
that it's only make-believe

oh, it's such a sneaky rotten thing
I'm *sure* the C.P.R. invented Spring!

21

The Sumter & Choctaw Railway Company

O.E. Hanson, Director—President
W.F. Jackson, Director—Vice President & General Manager
J.W. Bard, Director—Treasurer
C.R. Pederson, Secretary
R. H. Lorenz, Director
C.L. Poland, Director
C.D. French, Director—Assistant Secretary
H.G. Duren, Assistant Secretary & Assistant Treasurer
T.L. Johnston, Assistant Treasurer

Miles of road operated—3.55
Locomotives—diesel electric—1
Freight cars—None

2. Rip and Back Shop

old country letter   1932

vun day foreman call me over
say he got letter for me
from old country

I no vanna leesen heem
I know vat dis mean it
old country letter

mean you laid off
feenish

I tell heem
prosho pani
beg on my knee
for he let me stay

he just laugh on me
say   veentor comin
you got no family   no English
you vanna drive d' spike
cost you tventy dollar

an' bottle veesky
every payday

the interpreter

ve lay it d' steel
and dey bring us
d' bunch Portuguese
can't any speak it d' English
not von vord
don't know even
d' east from vest

bot dey know it
vat direction is d' Vinnipeg
and vat direction is d' Wancouwer
so every time ve vant move it d' rail
ve holler dem

yo!   Vinnipeg!
yo!   Wancouwer!

steam days

long before
management by objective was invented
everybody knew better
than to run into Old Billy
head on

Billy was old-time railroad
right down to the red kerchief
round his neck
plow-steel mean
rough as the coal in his tender
he worked his firemen hard
but he always brought his train in
right on time
never ran his boiler dry

so the time
Billy got all riled up
about two speed tests back to back
swore he'd work to rule
until the day he retired
the dispatcher wired a message
for the Operator at Madison Lake
to hand up to Billy
on Number 62

Extra 2634 North
pass No 62 Eng 2618
when overtaken

Old Billy read the orders
grunted
spat a fine brown stream
out the window
had his wheels spinning
before the train order signal cleared

Get shovellin he said
no goddamn extra's gonna scoop us!
Sonofabitchin dispatcher
knows that, too!

on the old outfit

gagging on the stench of unwashed feet
in the close tight darkness of the bunk car
Doogan rose exhausted from his bed
to find Wikowski sitting happily
soothing his aching feet
in a bucket of hot water
and Doogan
recognizing the bucket
as the same potato pail
the cook used to soak
each meal's white peeled spuds
broke Wikowski's nose
more in envy than in anger

the baggage room

used to be
the baggage man locked up
and went home for dinner

lot of people would come round the back
hoping to find someone there
the pipe-fitter's shop was right next door
with just a partition
the top an open space
between us and the baggage room
one day at noon we're in the shop, having lunch
when we hear a rattle at the baggage room door
and some guy knocking, asking *Anybody there?*
naturally we can hear just like
we're in the baggage room itself
so Don yells *Whatdya want?*
I want somebody to open the door the guy says
You got a broken arm? he yells at the guy
Open it yourself!

for a minute there's silence
then the guy says, real calm
Look, I wanna check this trunk.
So bring it in! Don says
I can't! the guy yells *The goddamn door's locked!*
Don yells back, real smart
Guess that's just your tough luck!

at last the guy catches on
What are you, some kinda smart ass? he yells
Smarter'n you! Don shouts
You can't even get the goddamn door open!

Jeez, the guy goes wild, kicking the door and swearing
You dirty sonofabitch! he's almost crying he's so mad
I get this door open I'll break your bloody neck!

he goes away and we start worrying now
he's gonna get in his car and ram the door
but then we hear him take off
tires just a-screaming

around quitting time
we drop by the baggage room
ask Nick *How's it going?*

Christ he says
I don't know what the world's coming to.
Some guy barges in here with a trunk, cursing
threatening to bust me in the nose.
Never seen him before in my life!
Had a hell of a time to calm him down.
Big bastard, too!
I don't know, this goddamn job.
Goddamn crazy public!

the Christian railroader

lunchtime is the usual
sandwiches and hockey
when this guy walks in
suit and briefcase
says he's got permission
from the foreman
starts right in
about how he's witnessin
at every rip and back shop
in the country

well, he ain't doin us no harm
except everybody's kinda nervous
so we stare into our lunch pails
and listen to him go on

BROTHAHS he says
and you AH muh brothahs
Ah'm heah to spread the gospel of sweeet
JESUS CHRIST
and to let you KNOW
that GAWD is WITH you
HEAH on the job
NOT just in church
YESSIR BROTHAHS GAWD'S beSIDE you
whethah you be in OVAH-ALLS
or wearin yoah SUNDAY BEST

every time he shouts
I almost choke
on the hardboiled egg I'm trying to eat

then I'll be go to hell
if he don't bust out singin

ROCK A AGES
CLEFT FOR ME

not too bad a voice, either
and when he stops it's real quiet
everybody sittin there lookin dopey
not knowin whether to clap or what

Jeez, the guy
has more guts n' a slaughterhouse!

I doubt if he saved anybody, though
cause the minute he's gone
we're back at it
Leaf fans cursin the Frogs
somebody else gettin in
about the Sabres or the Islanders
and the hockey season still two months away

Detroit 3   Leafs 1

I'm in the van
waiting for the air
and he's lighting his markers
when I just happen to mention
I heard on the news
Jack Benny died

NO!!!

he whirls around   the match
still lit in his hand

DEAD!
THE HELL, YOU SAY!
JACK BENNY?

. . . well, it was on the . . .

GOD-DAMN, EH?
JACK BENNY!
DEAD, YOU SAY!

. . . it must be true . . .

JACK BENNY!
GONE!
HARD TO BELIEVE, EH?
EH?

. . . uh, yeah, hard to believe . . .

JUST SEEN HIM THE OTHER NIGHT ON TV!
AND YOU SAY HE'S DEAD!
GOD, THAT'S A CRIME, EH?
HOW OLD WAS HE, ANYWAY?

I dunno . . . thirty-nine, I guess . . .

GOD!
THIRTY-NINE, EH?
DEAD, EH?
WHAT KILLED HIM? CANCER?
PROBABLY CANCER, EH?

. . . probably . . .

AW, THEM DOCTORS
THEY'LL TELL YOU THEY CAN CURE IT
BUT THEY DON'T KNOW, EH?
CANCER, EH?
JACK BENNY, EH?

at last
the gauge on the wall reads 65 lbs.
I get up
to give his train a brake test

BE SEEIN' YOU!
THAT'S SURE A BUGGER
ABOUT POOR OLD JACK BENNY
EH?

he stops me at the door

SAY, YOU BEEN LISTENIN' TO THE RADIO
HOW'D THE LEAFS MAKE OUT TONIGHT?

glass houses

the shack
stifling hot
against the winter night
& Butch the switch foreman
stretched out along the bench
engages his companions
in after-dinner conversation

no wonder my taxes
are so goddamn high
this morning I went down for my cheque
it was barely after nine
two city trucks
were already parked outside the restaurant
streets full of holes
and they're sittin on their asses
drinkin coffee

someone grunts
head nodding in the heat
goes back to his *Penthouse*

outside
the quarter-million dollar goat
idles monotonously
rattling the window pane
every fifteen seconds

Butch yawns   stretches
dreams of better days
in a workers' paradise

Railways have their own versions of the "Kilroy was here!" graffiti of World War II. These creations of unknown artists are often unique and imaginative. Railway cars, always on the move, are natural vehicles for these self-advertisements.

al fresco

scrawled on countless box cars
yellow crayon drawings
    of the little man
      asleep beneath his enormous sombrero
    in the shade of a palm
roll through every rail yard
up and down the seaboard
on the coast
and in between

Herby is by far
the most prolific
of those anonymous celebrities
the box car artists
and if you've worked the rails awhile
you can tell the real Herbies
from the forgeries,
cite the chronological order
of his appearance
in relation to Thirty and Out
or Fred & Irma's Ninth Street Bar and Grill,
with a fine eye classify Early Herbies
from his Modern Blue Period,
disdain the Bubbler
for his lack of originality,
appreciate the one-upmanship
of turning the Rambler's
martini glass over
and signing it
Thanks, Rambler!

C.P.R. Hungarian rhapsody

I see it, sonofabitch
but I can't believe it
on mine own eyes
how them analops
mixin in with the deerses
we hidin behind some elmer trees
and I get into the poison ivory
isn't it?
anyway, I get so excited
I forget to shoot
and they all runaway

then when we comin back
we listen on radio
Rosh-ins and Canadian
play World Serious
and just when I drive
over that sweet clover north of town
this cop he stop me
tell me I drive
with intensive care
I tell him no I not
but he let me go anyway

yesterday I go to the Buffalo Lake fishin
and some Dutchmans and Frenchmans was there
boy, they ever speak the broken English
I hardly understand it them
but what the hell
it's a free country
don't it?

3. Wrecking

the secret life of railroaders

the s.a.p. call
comes at 4 a.m.
and in the taxi, half-asleep
he thinks about

> his office
> dark now
> just a small red glow marking
> the location of the fire extinguisher
> light reflecting
> softly off the panelled walls
> the clock ticking

ice crystals in the air
& the auxiliary coupled up
men checking boxes/the brake test
thirty-five in the ditch
this side of Brandon
grain   lumber   acid   butane
emergency response forms
MCB 23-B's & time sheets
whose first shift
to ride the idler

beyond Regina
streaks of sunrise in the sky
monotonous clickety-clack
the train swaying

> perhaps
> he would still be there
> at his desk
> lost in dusty archives
> startled when Miss Mason
> brings in morning coffee
> mock disapproval on her face
> later
> he might shave and stretch out
> on the leather couch
> his hours flexible

the first night is always
a nightmare painting by Hieronymous Bosch
huge front-end loaders rushing
back & forth like praying mantis
headlights gleaming
caterpillars clanking
over the tangled graveyard
two-inch cables tearing
wreckage into wreckage
men swarm
stunned in the noise
vulnerable

        he rises refreshed
        lunches in the university cafeteria
        there are no sectionmen eating here
        but two young girls
        his students
        come over to sit with him
        their legs smooth
        their faces smooth
        their breasts . . .
        they are attentive
        anxious to be impressed
        unaware of his association
        with cramped chemical toilets

eleven of the cars are burners
will be cut into scrap
the rest are dragged to the track
placed on wheels
hauled to the siding
for temporary repairs

by the time they are ready
to come home
it is snowing again

on the way back
some of the men sleep
some play rummy
he thinks about

        the essays
        piled on the desk
        waiting his return
        some will be on the awakening
          of young womanhood
        some on the recurring
          anthropomorphic theme in Can Lit
        there will be one on Kafka
        one on the Four Quartets
        none

will be about the railroad

he wonders

        how he will cope

at Grenfell

freight cars piled up
four and five high
like toys in a sandbox
spilling their lading
into a sea
of grain and fertilizer and sulphur
and splintered lumber

we got our first taste
of wrecking there
wading from sunrise to dark
through the mess
dragging cables
hauling blocks and ties
aching for home and a shower
and a change of clothes
unable to imagine the track
clear and straight
ever again

each night
we tossed sleepless
in our top bunks
wrapped in dirt and sweat
while the old-timers
played cards
or snored peacefully below

the third day out
we had lumberman's arch
walking like ducks
certain it was cancer of the rectum
suffering in embarrassed silence

but on the way back
with the tool car rocking
from side to side
slamming the hanging chains
against the wall
we counted our money
and wondered
where the next wreck would be

Every legend begins with some ordinary occurrence, like the time we stopped to inspect our train on our way to a wreck in a white-out blizzard. We bought cigarettes, not beer. However, the power of a legend lies not in what happened, but in the re-telling.

inspection stop at Rouleau

might just as well sit down, Jack
and have a drink
ain't nothin movin on the road tonight
highway's blocked an more snow comin
accordin to the radio
say, did I ever tell you
about the time —
why, thanks, don't mind if I do
make mine a double

it was a night like this
a little worse maybe
only reason I was here
I couldn't make it home
the roads so bad
I'd had a few
but Bert was here and Jesse
and the Andersons from east of town
— you remember, Cal
you were on the bar that night

it was near to closin time
I swear you could feel a chill
before the door opened
if it did open
all I know is all at once
they were standin there
white with snow and frost
dressed in parkas   muffled
couldn't hardly see their eyes
I don't remember hearin them speak
although they must have
because the next thing I know
Cal here was pilin 48 beer on the counter

— that's right, Cal, the exact amount!
god almighty
I don't know how you moved that night
my own legs like rubber

anyway
without a word
they moved toward the door
and the one
sort of turned in our direction
Jesus, it made my blood run cold

well, I ain't sayin what they were
and there's some things better left alone
but we watched them walk
into that howlin blizzard
disappear into the dark
beer and all

next day I called Earl
but they hadn't stopped there
and there's not another house for miles

oh, I ain't the only one seen them
Bert was here and Jesse and Cal
and the Andersons from east of town

by moonlight

the tank cars lie in snow
a school of killer whales
beached on white sands

dressed like eskimos
we've come to land them
with a 200-ton test line

level crossing

it is our business
to be at this place
we have an entire train
self-contained
a fortune in tools and equipment
the solution for
small indiscretions
like daydreaming for a moment
(the blonde last night
with nothing under her dress)

in the split-second difference
this way or that
Halley's comet reaches perihelion
turns in its ellipse to intercept
a planet not yet born

it is our business
to wait for what will happen
all that is left of the truck
lies on the highway
barely distinguishable from the load of scrap
it was carrying

someone reaches over
takes the key from the ignition
a souvenir   he says

FORM A   (Single Track)

Fixing Meeting Points for Opposing Trains

No 442 Eng 5792
meet Extra 8404 East at Winfield

Extra 8404 East take siding at Winfield

they found his orders
complete and repeated
folded in his overalls pocket
but when he came around that curve
and looked at 442's headlight
it would have been too late
to read them again

he wasn't asleep
because he plugged 'er
but hell, that's fast track
coming out of Winfield
and with 9,000 tons behind
it wouldn't even slow 'er down

he must have known
they weren't gonna make it
just hung on the whistle
rode 'er right into the other train

tail-end crew on 442 said
that whistle
was the most god-awful sound
they ever heard

at Balgonie

we came upon the body
quite by chance
although we knew it had to be there
beneath the twisted tons of steaming wreckage

a shapeless mound
yet unmistakably a man
a gray mummy wrapped in rags
smoking in its own ashes

three units and forty-one cars piled up in five pole lengths
meant nothing
we held our hard hats in our hands
and shuffled on the tread marks in the mud

we felt the wind of the sun going down
and the people at our backs surging forward
craning for a better look
while the constable tried to force them back
before some fool used his camera

watching wheels

gleaming black raincoats
gather in the circle of light
in front of the crane
and back here
in the dark
rain pelts monotonously on my hard hat
sends a river
down the back of my neck
every two minutes

what the hell are they doing?
Jeez, it seems to take forever
to truck a load
when you're stuck in this job
stretched out on the roadbed
watching for a crack of light
between the rail
and the crane's back wheels

not that it isn't important
if the crane tips over
we'll all be down the road
those of us who are still alive

Whatchya doin'?
the voice comes out of the dark
behind me

Christ, it isn't bad enough
lying here on the ground
at two in the morning
soaking wet
I really need this inevitable asshole
rubbernecking in the rain
asking me what I'm doing

Watching wheels I say
not taking my eyes off the rail

after a while
I hear him shrug in the dark
and walk away
his boots crunching on the ballast
toward the friendly light

mileage 60.5   Indian Head Sub.

sitting in the idler
stunned from lack of sleep
and the heat from the stove
I feel the slack run out
as we slow and jerk to a halt somewhere
in the moonless night

stretching, I stumble out on the deck
where the chill
brings the need to relieve myself
and I lean out into the blackness
when the sudden flood of light
and the angry warning horn
freeze all my bodily functions

I think of Doppler
and try to calculate
the force of 10,000 tons at 60 mph
as 949 hurtles by
the wheels sparking and skidding
steel on steel
and as I watch the bright red markers
of the tail-end
recede into the night
it comes to me
how ridiculous I must have looked
standing there   watering the turnips
as the saying goes

wrecking, in winter

we've come 3 miles
at a mile an hour
with this bent axle
threatening to throw its wheels
off the track
at every turn

the hard stars are ice
in the frozen night
over this dead planet
and to the south
cars race by on the highway
heaters on   radios playing
going home

I could walk over there
thumb a ride
nobody would leave a man
standing outside
on a night like this

but what the hell
we're just a hundred yards now
to the siding
if she don't jump off
at the switch
we'll get in clear
run around 'er
stick a new truck under the sonofabitch

then it's steak with fried potatoes
for breakfast
and lying in bed
with the sportscast
those first few moments
drifting in the warm heavy sea
as the morning sun
touches the frosted windows

traitor

I put my tools away
take a final look around
the rip track silent
in falling snow

but when I turn
to lock the tool box
the tommy bar has climbed back out

Twenty-five years together it says
the words hard as steel
and you'd leave without even saying good-bye

I wanted to, but —

That's longer than most marriages last!
Just goes to show
you never really know someone

Too good for us now the sledge grunts

Listen I say *be reasonable!*
I can't take you with me

We were good enough for him
when he had to earn a living
buy a home, raise a family the bar says
speaking as if I were already gone
How many thousand sill steps
did we straighten for him?
How many grab irons? How many boxes jacked?

Just remember, office boy the sledge booms
when you're sitting there in your 3-piece suit
your feet up on the desk
we won't be there to help you
And there'll be no union
for you to run to when you screw up!

chisels and hammers shout
chains rattle over the edge of the box
wrenches fling themselves at my shins

I stuff them back in the box
slam the lid and lock it

they hammer against the lid, howling
as I walk away

later, I clean out my locker
carry a pair of torn overshoes
and a greasy parka
to the garbage barrel

but I can't do it

and I tell them   *shut up*
hide them
in the trunk of my car

James S. McCanless owns ten covered hoppers

his friends golf
or walk their dogs
one has a stamp collection
they come by the house most afternoons
play checkers
pass the time of day

James S. McCanless
owns ten covered hoppers
5,250 cubic feet level full
has his initials
stencilled on the sides

each morning
he walks the half-mile to the track
inspects his cars
for brake shoe wear
bent ladder rungs   missing split keys
scans the straight square bodies
with a practiced eye

once in a great while
he finds a bad-order wheel
moving with the efficient patience
of his years
he jacks the car
replaces the condemned set
with a rusty new pair
careful to save the retainer bolts

the gardening
he leaves to his wife
that was her life-long passion

something in the blood

in the long afternoons
with his friends around him
making conversation
he listens to the singing
of the air in the reservoirs

railroader

hell, I was just a kid
when I hired on
green as new grass
but they taught me my trade
paid me to learn it
and if the work was hard
well, nobody promised any different

coulda fired me a dozen times
for horseplay and goofin off
full of piss and vinegar
when I was young
but if the foreman caught me
he'd just kick me in the ass
life was simple then

some would say
I never did amount to much
coulda been Chairman of the Board, I guess
if I'd a put my mind to it
worked right beside
the man who did
right here on the midnight shift
he still stops and says hello
whenever he comes through

it's been a good life
just the same
never had to take a nickel
from no one
kept my family fed
put the kids through school
my house
all bought and paid for

I'll be retiring next year
I've got my health
and the wife and I
will do some travelling

no, I can't complain
the way I see it
I coulda done a lot worse
than work for the railway

4. I Don't Write Poems for Railroaders

After a poetry reading one evening, I tagged along to the bar with six English teachers, who showed me there's no magic to becoming invisible.

I'd love to call them to double some night in D Yard. Three to five to twelve and cut the shorts in behind twenty.

sometimes I know how a woman feels
(for Gwen Currie)

around the table
in the pub
six English teachers
speak names
remote names/famous and obscure
speak   style
speak   technique
speak   metaphor
speak   Greek

Gwen
as you sit so quietly
it occurs to me at last
that you and I
are the only ones here
who don't have a moustache

Railway jargon is probably as confusing to mathematicians as the numbers game is to railroaders, but once in a while it's fun to play in the other guy's trainyard.

confounded poem
(for Ed Dyck)

once more
             you've left me
on the Penrose staircase
reduced to bones
while you meditate
the barren Cartesian plane

calculating
             the distance between us
by the height of the chandelier
you throw the Peano curve
and trip me on the stepping stones
of your
congruent convex polygons

I stumble
blind and groping
in the golden ratio
as you explain
how the sequence loops
with a period of five
the infinitesimals of nonstandard analysis
cardinals

enough of your damn Wang
dominoes!
omega!   I say
surely
you could be more understanding
than to hit me in the face
with pi

When I first began to attend poetry readings, I listened one evening as a very young female poet read from her work and I found myself thinking about the men I worked with. Men who had never written a line.

the poet

she tears open her robe
thinking it exposure
but I have seen young girls crying
in back seats of sedans
and women
drawing shades in darkened rooms

she gorges on blood-red meat
wallows in the sticky juice
of plucked ripe fruit
boldly wipes her mouth
with the back of her hand
I lived one long cold winter
with only potatoes to eat
and have no stomach now

she screams in my face
of dark places she has been
and of the soarings of her mind
though I remember
times I would have stopped the sun
from rising

someday
          she will look into the eyes
of a man made speechless
or see a bent and lonely woman
waiting for a bus
and will write a poem
to fold and wrinkle
until it no longer matters
that I cannot read the words

I've seen these bitter verses, over and over again, scrawled on the sides of box cars.

I don't write poems for railroaders

I don't write poems
for railroaders
they'd use them
to line their overshoes
roll them in balls
to plug their ears   against
those lonely crossing whistles
that make folk singers rich

> *up hill slow*
> *down hill fast*
> *tonnage first*
> *safety last*

they have learned
about the unions
the lies of government
and how the company
will spend five hundred dollars
to avoid paying
a dollar-forty meal ticket

> *drive those spikes*
> *and don't complain*
> *you don't get hired*
> *for your brain*

they spend
lives
along the snow fence
or in the shops
linked
shift to shift
year to year
father to son
they become the rails
lie down beneath the wheels

·

> *broken strikes*
> *and broken tools*
> *dirt and death*
> *and books of rules*

the smell of creosote
the gleaming yards at sunrise
the trembling power
of the diesels
are the poems
railroaders hold inside

they talk
of the day when they can leave
and stay
unable to go
unable to embrace
the thing
they love

The THUNDER CREEK CO-OP is a production co-operative registered with the Saskatchewan Department of Co-operatives and Co-operative Development. It was formed to publish prairie writing — poetry, prose, songs and plays.

PUBLICATIONS

SASKATCHEWAN GOLD, a powerful collection of short stories from the new west, edited by Geoffrey Ursell, $3.50.

THE SECRET LIFE OF RAILROADERS, the funniest poems ever to roll down the main line, by Jim McLean, $5.00.

EARTH DREAMS, startingly original poems by Jerry Rush, $5.00.

BLACK POWDER:ESTEVAN, 1931, a play with music by Rex Deverell and Geoffrey Ursell, $5.00.

SINCLAIR ROSS: A READER'S GUIDE by Ken Mitchell. With two stories by Sinclair Ross, $7.00.

ALL STAR POET, hockey poems by Stephen Scriver, $2.95

A NEW IMPROVED SKY, poems by Don Kerr, $5.00.

SUNDOGS, an anthology of the best in Saskatchewan short stories, edited by Robert Kroetsch, $7.95.

WILD MAN'S BUTTE, a dramatic poem set in Saskatchewan's Big Muddy, by Terrence Heath and Anne Szumigalski, $3.00

SUPERWHEEL, the musical play about automobiles, with script by Rex Deverell and music and lyrics by Geoffrey Ursell, $5.00.

NUMBER ONE HARD, an L.P. of the songs by Geoffrey Ursell from the original Globe Theatre production, "an investigative documentary about the prairie grain industry," $6.00.

NUMBER ONE NORTHERN, an anthology of Saskatchewan poetry. Winner of the 1978 Saskatchewan Publishing Prize, $7.00.

EYE OF A STRANGER, poems by Garry Raddysh, $4.00.

ODPOEMS &, poems by E.F. Dyck, $4.00.

GHOST HOUSE, stories and poems by Lois Simmie, $3.00.

MOVING IN FROM PARADISE, poems by Mick Burrs, $3.00.

HOME STREET, poems by Gary Hyland, $2.00.

MOVING OUT, poems by Robert Currie, $2.00.

PRAIRIE GRASS, PRAIRIE SKY, an L.P. with songs by Rob Bryanton, Bob Evans, Glenn Koudelka, Connie Kaldor, and Geoffrey Ursell, $7.00.

All of the above may be ordered from

THUNDER CREEK CO-OP
Box 239, Sub #1
Moose Jaw, Saskatchewan
S6H 5V0